Learning to Read, Step by Step!

Ready to Read   Preschool–Kindergarten
• big type and easy words • rhyme and rhythm • picture clues
For children who know the alphabet and are eager to begin reading.

Reading with Help   Preschool–Grade 1
• basic vocabulary • short sentences • simple stories
For children who recognize familiar words and sound out new words with help.

Reading on Your Own   Grades 1–3
• engaging characters • easy-to-follow plots • popular topics
For children who are ready to read on their own.

Reading Paragraphs   Grades 2–3
• challenging vocabulary • short paragraphs • exciting stories
For newly independent readers who read simple sentences with confidence.

Ready for Chapters   Grades 2–4
• chapters • longer paragraphs • full-color art
For children who want to take the plunge into chapter books but still like colorful pictures.

STEP INTO READING® is designed to give every child a successful reading experience. The grade levels are only guides; children will progress through the steps at their own speed, developing confidence in their reading. The F&P Text Level on the back cover serves as another tool to help you choose the right book for your child.

Remember, a lifetime love of reading starts with a single step!

Thank you, Heidi Kilgras,
for giving me the opportunity to "power up"—
you are amazing! And, as always, thank you, Nancy.

For my mother and father, who came to
Canada and made it their home
—M.K.

To my grandparents
—V.F.

Text copyright © 2017 by Monica Kulling
Cover art and interior illustrations copyright © 2017 by Valerio Fabbretti

All rights reserved. Published in the United States by Random House Children's Books,
a division of Penguin Random House LLC, New York.

Step into Reading, Random House, and the Random House colophon are registered trademarks of
Penguin Random House LLC.

Visit us on the Web!
StepIntoReading.com
randomhousekids.com

Educators and librarians, for a variety of teaching tools, visit us at RHTeachersLibrarians.com

Library of Congress Cataloging-in-Publication Data
Names: Kulling, Monica, author. | Fabbretti, Valerio, illustrator.
Title: Alexander Hamilton : from orphan to founding father / by Monica Kulling ;
illustrated by Valerio Fabbretti.
Description: New York : Random House, 2017. | Series: Step into reading. Step 3
Identifiers: LCCN 2016029613 (print) | LCCN 2016029851 (ebook) |
ISBN 978-1-5247-1698-1 (trade pbk.) | ISBN 978-1-5247-1699-8 (hardcover library binding) |
ISBN 978-1-5247-1700-1 (ebook)
Subjects: LCSH: Hamilton, Alexander, 1757–1804—Juvenile literature. |
Statesmen—United States—Biography—Juvenile literature. | United States—Politics and
government—1783–1809—Juvenile literature.
Classification: LCC E302.6.H2 K85 2017 (print) | LCC E302.6.H2 (ebook) | DDC 973.4092 [B]—dc23

Printed in the United States of America
10 9 8 7 6 5 4 3 2 1

This book has been officially leveled by using the F&P Text Level Gradient™ Leveling System.

STEP 3 INTO READING®

STEP 3 READING ON YOUR OWN

A BIOGRAPHY READER

Alexander Hamilton
From Orphan to Founding Father

by Monica Kulling
illustrated by Valerio Fabbretti

Random House 🏠 New York

All hands on deck!
A ship's crew rushed
to put out a fire.

Days later,

the burned ship

docked at Boston Harbor.

Young Alexander Hamilton

had been at sea for three weeks.

He was restless and ready

to start a new life.

It was 1773.

Alexander Hamilton
was born in 1755
on Nevis,
an island in the Caribbean
(ka-ruh-BE-yun).

His father left

when Alex was a boy.

Three years later,

while living on St. Croix,

Alex's mother died.

Alex was now an orphan

with nothing.

Alex got work as a clerk

in a company that traded

with New England,

in America.

He learned

about money and business.

When the boss placed him
in charge for six months,
Alex ran the company
as though it were his own.
He was only
fourteen years old.

In 1772,

a hurricane hit the islands.

Roaring winds tore up trees

and blew away houses.

Alex wrote about the storm,

and his account was published

in the local newspaper.

Some rich businessmen
liked the way Alex wrote.
They decided to send him
to college in America.

When Alex arrived in America,
there were thirteen colonies.
England ruled America
and taxed everything—
books, sugar, coffee, paint. . . .

The colonists wanted the right
to make their own taxes and
to have a say in
how their money was spent.
Alex was at King's College
in New York
the night rebel colonists
took action in Boston.

The king of England was mad.

He closed Boston Harbor

to punish the colonists.

King George sent in soldiers.

Redcoats crowded the streets!

Alex became a patriot.

He gave speeches

about the need to end British rule.

As a boy,

Alex had read about

wars that brought change.

War might be the only way

for America

to break free of England.

On April 19, 1775,

British soldiers marched

into Lexington, Massachusetts.

The patriots stood their ground.

No one knows who fired

the first shot,

but the American Revolution

had begun.

After college,

Alex joined the army.

Captain Alexander Hamilton

loved to drill his troops.

"Right flank . . . march!"

On Bayard's Mount,
the highest point
in Lower Manhattan,
Alex and his men
got ready for battle.

The Founding Fathers had written
the Declaration of Independence.
It stated that the colonies
no longer belonged to England.

On July 9, 1776,
General Washington read it aloud
to soldiers in New York.
Captain Hamilton was proud.
Thirteen gunshots rang out—
one for each state.
In New York Harbor,
British battleships waited.

The British ships began firing.

BOOM!

Captain Hamilton ordered
his soldiers to fire back.

BOOM!

Hour after hour,

cannons exploded.

Smoke and noise choked the air.

Captain Hamilton
knew the British Navy
was powerful.
They had more guns and men
than the patriot army.

The British captured Brooklyn!
General George Washington ordered
people to leave the city.

Washington had seen
Captain Hamilton in action.
He asked him to be
his personal secretary.

Hamilton had to think about it.

He wanted to be in battle!

But he could not refuse

the great General Washington.

Hamilton wrote
letters to Congress
to ask for more supplies
for the army.
He was a fine writer.
He would do this job for years.
But Hamilton never quit asking
to fight again.
He got his chance in 1781.

The British were dug in
at Yorktown, Virginia.
They had built ten barriers
to protect their position.

Numbers nine and ten
were near American lines.
They were the weakest.
Hamilton was ordered
to attack number ten.

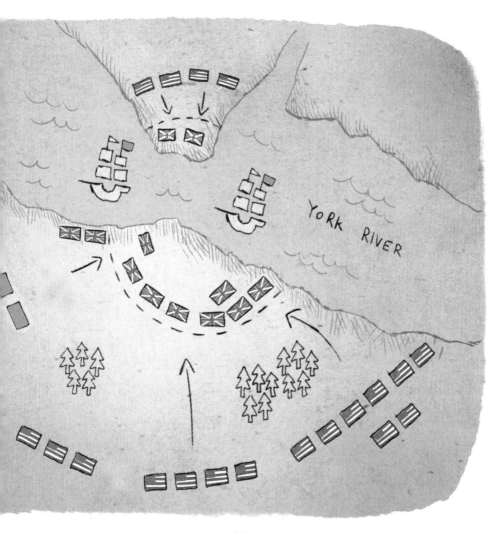

Hamilton led the charge.

"Let's get 'em, boys!" he shouted.

He raced across open ground.

He leaped over the barricades.

He fought hard and with courage.

The British were beaten.

The Battle of Yorktown

ended the war.

Hamilton was a hero.

It was 1782.

Hamilton left the army

and lived in Lower Manhattan.

He was now a husband,

a lawyer, and a father.

But he still worried about his country.

The states were in trouble.

They didn't work together.

They had no money.

Hamilton thought about
some of the books he had read.

The early Greeks and Romans
wrote about how to build a city,
run a government,
and take care of the citizens.
Hamilton knew the states
had to form a union
or they would not survive.

The states needed a set of laws.
These laws would become
the Constitution.
Hamilton attended months
of meetings in Philadelphia
to work on the document.

At least nine states
had to accept it
to make it the law.

Hamilton wanted voters
in New York State
to understand the Constitution.
He and two other men wrote
many essays that were
published in newspapers.
Hamilton wrote most
of what came to be called
the Federalist Papers.

Voters now understood
and accepted the Constitution.

The states were one nation!

People in New York celebrated

with a parade.

A ship on wheels

called the *Hamilton*

was pulled down Broadway.

Alexander Hamilton,

an immigrant,

had helped steer

his adopted home

into forming a union.

Now it was time to build

the new nation.

The United States of America
needed a leader.
The people chose
General Washington
to be the first president.
President Washington
chose Alexander Hamilton to be
the secretary of the treasury.

Hamilton was smart with money.

He helped set up the first

national bank,

with one national currency,

or money system.

Alexander Hamilton
always had very strong opinions.
He wrote articles about some of
the men who ran the government,
calling them awful names.

One of the men, Aaron Burr,
challenged Hamilton
to a gunfight called a duel.

At dawn on July 11, 1804,

in Weehawken, New Jersey,

the pair stood face to face.

Hamilton shot to miss.

Burr shot to kill.

Hamilton died the next day.

Alexander Hamilton's life

is a real rags-to-riches story.

He came to America with nothing,

but quickly found himself

in the middle of making

a new country.

Hamilton's story is one of daring,

hard work,

and ideas.

It still inspires us today.